The Marshall Cavendish Collection of

# GREEN & PLE
## ·WALK

GN00374226

# *The Coast*
# *of Cornwall*

## MARSHALL CAVENDISH

First published in Great Britain in 1997 by
Marshall Cavendish Books, London
(a division of Marshall Cavendish Partworks Ltd).

Copyright © Marshall Cavendish Ltd 1997

ISBN 1-85435-879-0

British Library Cataloguing in Publication Data:
A catalogue record for this book is available from the British Library

Printed and bound in Italy

Some of this material has previously appeared in the
Marshall Cavendish partwork *Out and About.*

Picture Credits
Andrew Besley  pages 9, 12, 24, 25, 29, 40. Andrew Cleave/ Nature Photographers Ltd  page 36. Mary Evans Picture Library  page16. Derek Forss  page 33, 37. Ray Grange  page 13. R. Hillgrove / National Trust Photo Library  page 44. Rob Matheson / National Trust Photo Library  page 21. Alan North / National Trust Photo Library  page 41. Royal Navy Dockyards Museum  page 8. Mike Williams  pages 5, 17, 20. All other pictures: Marshall Cavendish Picture Library

Art Editor: Joyce Mason
Designer: Richard Shiner
Editor:  Irena Hoare
Picture Researcher: Vimu Patel
Production: Joanna Wilson

# CONTENTS

# GREEN & PLEASANT —— WALKS ——

The walks in *GREEN & PLEASANT WALKS* will give you ideas for walks near your own neighbourhood, as well as in other areas of Britain.

All the walks are devised around a theme, and range in length from about 2 to 9 miles (3.25 to 14.5km). They vary in difficulty from very easy to mildly strenuous, and since each walk is circular, you will always end up back at your starting point.

Background information is given for many of the walks, relating legends, pointing out interesting buildings, giving details about famous people who have lived in the area. There are occasional 'Nature Facts' panels, which highlight some of the things you might see in the landscape as you walk.

### THE LAW OF TRESPASS

If you find a right of way barred, the law says you may remove the obstruction, or take a short detour.

If the path is blocked by a field of crops, you may walk along the line of the path through the crops in single file. However, in England and Wales, if you stray from the path you are trespassing, and could be sued for damages.

If you do find that your path has been obstructed in some way, report the matter to the local authority, who will take the necessary action to clear the route.

It is illegal for farmers to place a bull on its own in a field crossed by a right of way (unless the bull is not a recognized dairy breed), but if you come across a bull on its own in a field, find another way round – and if you feel sufficiently aggrieved, report the farmer.

### USING MAPS

Although this book of *GREEN & PLEASANT WALKS* gives you all the information you need to enjoy your walks, it is useful to have a larger scale map to give you detailed information about

## THE COUNTRY CODE

- Enjoy the countryside, and respect the life and work of its inhabitants
- Always guard against any risk of fire
- Fasten all gates
- Keep your dogs under close control
- Keep to public footpaths across farmland
- Use gates and stiles to cross fences, hedges etc

- Leave livestock, crops and machinery alone
- Take your litter home with you
- Help to keep all water clean and unpolluted
- Protect wildlife, plants and trees
- Take special care on country roads
- Do not make any unnecessary noise

# THE COAST OF CORNWALL

**①** Prospect of Plymouth  **⑥** Lamorna Cove

**②** Ferry across the Fowey  **⑦** At the Edge of Land's End

**③** Tales of the Deadman  **⑧** Atlantic Headland

**④** Point to Point  **⑨** In Search of Camelot

**⑤** Frenchman's Creek  **⑩** Heritage Coast

*All walks featured in this book are plotted and numbered on the regional map below, and listed in the box (left).*

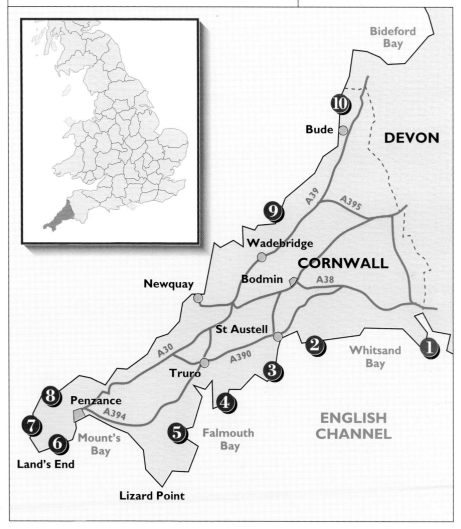

3

## The Coast of Cornwall

where you are. Britain is fortunate in having the best mapping agency in the world, the Ordnance Survey, which produces high-quality maps. The most useful of these for walkers are the 1:25,000 Pathfinder, Explorer and Outdoor Leisure maps. Use the grid references given in the fact files to help you find the starting point of each of the walks.

# GRID REFERENCES

All Ordnance Survey maps are over-printed with a framework of squares, called the National Grid. This is a reference system which, by breaking the country down into squares, lets you pinpoint an area and give it a unique number.

On OS Landranger, Pathfinder and Outdoor Leisure maps, a reference to an accuracy of 100m is possible. Grid squares on the maps cover an area of 1km x 1km on the ground.

### GRID REFERENCES

Blenheim Palace, in Oxfordshire, has a grid reference of **SP 441 161**. This is constructed as follows:

**SP:** These letters identify the 100km grid square in which Blenheim Palace lies. The squares form the basis of the National Grid. Information on the 100km square covering any given map is given in the map key.

**441 161:** This reference locates the position of Blenheim Palace to 100m in the 100km grid square.

**44:** This part of the reference is the number of the grid line which forms the western (left-hand) boundary of the 1km grid square in which Blenheim Palace appears. It is printed in the top and bottom margins of the relevant map (Pathfinder 1092 here).

**16:** This part of the reference is the number of the grid line which forms the southern boundary of the 1km grid square in which Blenheim Palace appears. The number is printed in the left and

right-hand margins of the relevant OS map (Pathfinder 1092 here).

Both numbers together (SP 4416) locate the bottom left-hand corner of the 1km grid square in which the Palace appears. The last figures in the reference **441 161** pinpoint the position in the square; dividing its western boundary lines into tenths and estimating on which imaginary tenths line the Palace lies.

# A Prospect of Plymouth

## A Cornish peninsula overlooking
## Devon's greatest city

*The folly in Mount Edgcumbe Park commands dramatic views across Plymouth Sound.*

From the high ground of Mount Edgcumbe Country Park there are spectacular views over the water to the historic city of Plymouth. Countless vessels, from rowing boats to naval warships, ply the deep channels of Plymouth Sound. The waterfront hubbub of the city dominates the scene, but never spoils the tranquillity of the park.

A day could happily be spent in Mount Edgcumbe's historic gardens, but there are other delights on the Maker Peninsula. To see these you set off round the estate on the coastal path, then after Kingsand climb up to Maker's church. You descend through Pigshill Wood to Empacombe Quay, then follow the coast to the ferry at Cremyll, a link to Plymouth for 600 years.

# THE WALK

## CREMYLL–KINGSAND

The walk begins in the car park just off the B3247 at Cremyll.

1 Turn left on main road. After 150 yards (135m), turn right through gate to Mount Edgcumbe Park **A**, then left towards building with arch. Go through, past orangery. Keep left, between hedges, to coast path. Pass fort.

2 At the amphitheatre, cross lawn to path, which ascends into wood. About 200 yards (180m) on, a folly **B** can be seen on right. Go through high gate; ignore fork to left. Follow marked path. The next mark points ahead, but main path forks right. Follow waymark to small path to head of beach. Beyond beach, grass path climbs to wider path. Turn left. Fence with 'Danger' sign bars way, but steps hard right zigzag up hill to gate. Go through. Path soon joins wide track. Turn left and under ivy-covered arch. Continue inland behind Fort Pickle-combe **C**, to shady grotto.

3 Follow path back to coast. After 500 yards (450m), go through two gates to stile on left.

4 Cross stile, down steps and right into lane. Soon, cross stile on left, take path to Cawsand for 1 mile (1.6km), reaching gate at Kingsand **D**.

5 Bear left towards Rising Sun, then turn sharp right to Lower Row to junction with Fore Street. Turn right for about 100 yards (90m).

6 Turn right into lane, Earl's Drive. After 3/4 mile (1.2km), beyond farm buildings, turn right, signed Pickle-combe, for short way.

7 Turn left on path to Maker's church, following telegraph poles. Cross two fields to Manor. Cross drive to path on left of house. Cross stile. With hedge on left go to next stile in field corner. Cross, hedge on right, to stile near church **E**. At church wall, turn left. Cross drive further on. Follow signed path over field to road.

8 Turn right. About 100 yards (90m) along is St Julian's Well **F**. Return up road, turn right on path signed Empa-combe. Follow waymark right, take lower right path at next junction. Cross field to gate to lane.

9 Cross to stile oppo-site, follow path to Empacombe Quay **G**. Follow edge of quay past pink house on corner to right. Where road bears right, go through gate to path ahead. Follow wall to gate into field. Cross stile on other side, follow path beside wire fence, over stile, through trees. At junction, bear left on track to lane. Bear right at fork to Cremyll Ferry **H**. Turn right to car park.

6

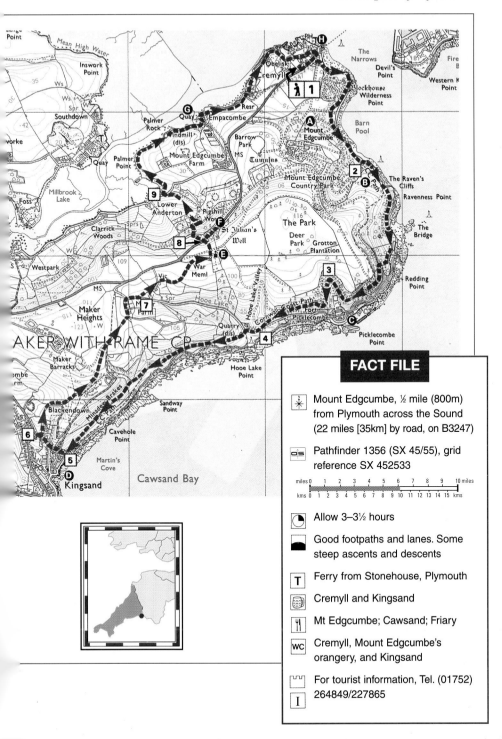

**FACT FILE**

Mount Edgcumbe, ½ mile (800m) from Plymouth across the Sound (22 miles [35km] by road, on B3247)

Pathfinder 1356 (SX 45/55), grid reference SX 452533

miles 0 1 2 3 4 5 6 7 8 9 10 miles
kms 0 1 2 3 4 5 6 7 8 9 10 11 12 13 14 15 kms

Allow 3–3½ hours

Good footpaths and lanes. Some steep ascents and descents

Ferry from Stonehouse, Plymouth

Cremyll and Kingsand

Mt Edgcumbe; Cawsand; Friary

Cremyll, Mount Edgcumbe's orangery, and Kingsand

For tourist information, Tel. (01752) 264849/227865

# Devonport Dockyards

*This engraving, which dates from the early 18th century, shows Mount Edgcumbe in the foreground.*

The story of the town of Devonport began towards the end of the 16th century, when the West Country man Sir Walter Raleigh recognized the potential of the site on the Hamoaze.

It was left to William of Orange, 100 years later, to begin building — perhaps out of gratitude to the people of Plymouth, who had been among the first to support him in his successful bid for the throne in 1688. The yard was designed by Edmund Dummer, and it soon became necessary to expand beyond his original 24-acre (10-ha) site. The new dock-workers, formerly housed in ships, soon needed more permanent housing, and this marked the foundation of the town of Plymouth Dockyard. Residents of Plymouth proper were not impressed, and regarded the new arrivals as riff-raff.

In 1824, however, the dockyard town gained its own identity, with royal approval, as Devonport. By 1837 its population had outstripped that of Plymouth itself.

The Great Breakwater across Plymouth Sound was started in 1812 and finished in 1840. By the mid-19th century, fears of invasion led Lord Palmerston to order the building of a ring of massive defences around the entrance to the harbour. Many of the old forts and batteries remain today.

Devonport's contribution to the local economy continues. Thirteen docks cover 2½ miles (4km) of waterfront, and employ 15,000 workers, a far cry from the 75 employed in 1691. Its continuing pre-eminence in the naval world now centres on the refitting of nuclear submarines.

# Ferry across the Fowey

## From a romantic novelist's village
## to views over the Fowey Estuary

*From Pont Pill Creek there is a clear view of St Catherine's Point in the distance.*

Bodinnick village overlooks the estuary of the River Fowey, and the view to its south-west is dominated by the town of Fowey on the opposite bank. Drowned by land-tilt long ago, the river valley forms a natural deepwater sheltered harbour that is home to countless yachts and is part of an important sea-faring highway. Nearly two million tons of valuable china clay are shipped out of this estuary each year.

The village owes its existence to the water, its motor ferry carrying people and cars regularly across the Fowey. A ferry was recorded here as far back as 1344, and was then a vital link in the old, southern route through Cornwall, carrying livestock and large consignments of beer. Ferry

*Continued on p. 12* ➤

9

# THE WALK

## BODINNICK–CARNE HILL

The walk begins at the free public car park just outside Bodinnick on the main approach road to the ferry.

**1** Take the road down the hill to come to the ferry. Leaving the waterside, turn uphill past the Old Ferry Inn **A** on your left. Further up, a plaque on the side-wall of Hall Walk cottage marks the way up a narrow footpath to Hall Walk.

**2** Continue along the path, which leads towards Penleath Point. Here, at the Quiller-Couch monument **B**, bear left alongside Pont Pill Creek until you reach a wooden stile. Cross it and turn right, keeping close to the hedge. When you come to an old slate cattle-grid, cross it and follow the path as it swings down to a junction. Take the signposted route right towards Polruan, dropping down to Pont Quay **C**.

**3** Cross the creek by means of a wooden footbridge, and take the uphill path next to Pont Creek Cottage. At the top, concrete steps lead onto a small road. Turn left.

**4** After a few strides, turn right into the lane next to Pont Poultry Farm; continue to the white gate into St Wyllow's churchyard **D**. Turn left through graveyard near the church door, and left again. Go through gate to Saffron Lane, opposite Churchtown Farm.

**5** Continue up the hill along the green lane for about 300 yards (270m). When you come to a fork, bear left. Where the lane splits again, keep to the right and continue until the lane peters out into a field.

**6** Keep the field hedge to your right to reach a wooden gate. Go through onto a narrow, overgrown path, which leads you to a road.

**7** Turn left. After 800 yards (720m) the road crosses the river downstream of Porthpean House **E**. Follow road signposted 'Pont', passing the remains of a smithy and limekiln, to Lombard Mill **F**. Fork right, then right again, taking path uphill to rejoin Hall Walk and return to cattle-grid.

**8** Head diagonally across the field on the other side of the grid (this path is easy to miss when crops are growing) and through the gate in the far left-hand corner. Walk through two fields, with hedge to your right. At the next field, the path crosses to the other side of the hedge and leads down to Hall Farm **G**.

**9** Continue, leaving farmyard on your right, into field. Cross stile at far side to meet up with Hall Walk. Turn right to return to the start.

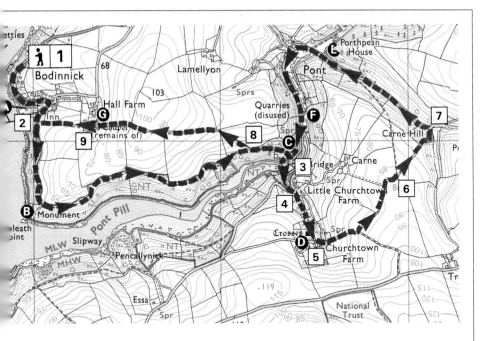

Cormorant chick, and adult bird drying its wings

## FACT FILE

☀ Bodinnick, 6½ miles (10.4km) east of St Austell

🖭 Pathfinder 1354 (SX 05/15), grid reference SX 129523

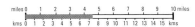

miles 0 1 2 3 4 5 6 7 8 9 10 miles

kms 0 1 2 3 4 5 6 7 8 9 10 11 12 13 14 15 kms

◖ Allow 3 hours

◼ Mostly good paths. Some short, steep ascents and descents. Mud in parts in wet weather. Fields with crops can be wet

P Free car park to left of approach to ferry; look for 'Ferry Queue' sign

T Foot and vehicle ferry from Fowey; for details, and tourist information,

I Tel. (01726) 833616

▦ The Old Ferry Inn, Bodinnick

rights were once owned by the local Mohun family. Later, rights passed to the Passage House Inn, now the Old Ferry Inn. As you walk to the ferry, look for a house called Ferryside beyond the slipway. This was once the home of the novelist Daphne du Maurier, and is still owned by the family. It was here that she wrote her first novel, *The Loving Spirit.*

Leaving the waterside, the walk up Bodinnick Hill passes the picturesque Old Ferry Inn **A**. Further up, a plaque on the wall of Hall Walk Cottage shows the way onto the historic Hall Walk, a private promenade through woods and across a creek, created by the Mohun family in the 16th century. Charles I, walking here during the Civil War siege of Fowey, saw one of his men killed by a musket shot fired from across the river.

*This old limekiln at Pont Quay is a reminder of a past industry.*

**Novelist's Memorial**

At the confluence of the River Fowey and Pont Pill Creek stands a monument **B** to the writer and scholar Sir Arthur Quiller-Couch. He is famous for his novels, in which Fowey is 'Troy', and he compiled the *Oxford Book of English Verse.*

The thick woodland that clothes the slopes of Pont Pill is surprisingly recent.

Until 100 years ago, the steep hillsides were grazed, but a change in land management has led to a natural regeneration of oak, ash, beech and sycamore.

The route passes a heronry in the woods and, as you drop down the hill from Hall Walk to the sleepy hamlet of Pont Quay **C**, you may see buzzards and nesting swans. By crossing a wooden footbridge that links the stone quays on either side of the creek and ascending the hill ahead, you come to the lovely church **D** at Lanteglos-by-Fowey. Much of the church dates from the 14th century, but a few Norman fragments survive.

When the path crosses a river via a bridge, look upstream to Porthpean House **E**, which was first recorded in 1331. Further along, the remains of a smithy and a limekiln, and Lombard Mill **F**, which dates from 1298, tell of the industry of a thriving local community that has long gone.

Climbing out of Pont the going gets tougher, rising to over 300 feet (90m). Below, Hall Farm **G** sits on the site of the old Manor of the Mohuns, destroyed in the Civil War, although part of the 14th-century chapel still remains. Beyond Hall Farm, the path drops to the start of Hall Walk.

# Tales of the Deadman

## A walk on country lanes and along a thrilling clifftop path

*An outcrop of thrift-covered rock is a colourful point on the Dodman's craggy coast.*

This walk to the wild headland of the Dodman (locally known as the 'deadman', *see page 16*) takes in some fine coastal scenery, although it takes a while to leave the houses of Gorran Haven behind. As you get closer to Gorran Churchtown, however, reminders of the present begin to slip away. When you cross the tabletop landscape, you will see many stone stiles, topped with granite columns laid on their sides. These are the remains of old field rollers.

The path undulates between sycamore, hawthorn and elder, with blackthorn providing protection from steep cliff edges. In places the ascent is hard, and the dizzying height is felt strongly at the Stone Cross, where the cliffs fall away to the crashing sea.

13

The Coast of Cornwall

# THE WALK

## GORRAN HAVEN–DODMAN POINT
The walk starts from Gorran
Haven's main car park.

**1** Turn right onto the road and follow for 1/2 mile (800m), to edge of village. Turn left on a footpath by a bench signposted Gorran (Churchtown). Cross stile and head diagonally across field to gap in far hedge. Head for left of white house, cross stile to road.

**2** Turn left. Where another road joins, keep right, through Gorran Churchtown. Go through village. Just beyond post office, turn left on footpath to Treveor. A few strides along, climb stile and cross two fields, hedge on right. Cross small lane, follow path opposite, signposted Treveor. By clump of trees on far side of field, climb stile to road.

**3** Turn left, then right. Pass Treveor Farm, ignoring footpaths signposted to Boswinger and Rescassa. Where road bends to right, turn left

over stile signposted to Tregavarras. Keep the cottages ahead of you to the right. Cross a footbridge, then a stile. Follow the path through a field, skirting gardens on the right, to another stile at the field gate. Follow cottage access track, continue on road.

**4** Where road bends sharp left, turn right by a cottage on a footpath marked 'Caerhays'. Follow a short track and climb the stile into open grassy field. Caerhays Castle **A** appears ahead. For a look at the castle, and for the beach, head for gate in bottom left hand corner of field. Otherwise, head in the same direction, but veer left before the bottom, to cross a stile next to a gate, on the left of the field.

**5** Follow coast path over a stile up steps. Pass Greeb Point **B**, drop to Hemmick Beach.

**6** Turn right on road; after 30 paces turn right over stile to coast path. After a gate, turn right, continue to crossing of paths at Dodman Point.

**7** Turn right to Stone Cross **C**. Retrace steps, follow path ahead. Dodman Watch House **D** appears. Continue to a stile into field. Keep left, by wire fence. Where this joins hedge, look left to see medieval strip field **E** by path. Go to gate in far left corner. To left, and just behind, is Bronze Age barrow. Through gate, path narrows to junction. Turn right, then right again over stile, to coast path. High bank to right is boundary **F** of Iron Age fort. Continue to junction.

**8** Turn left onto coast path. Go down steps into Gorran Haven's Foxhole Lane. At T-junction, turn left to return to the car park.

14

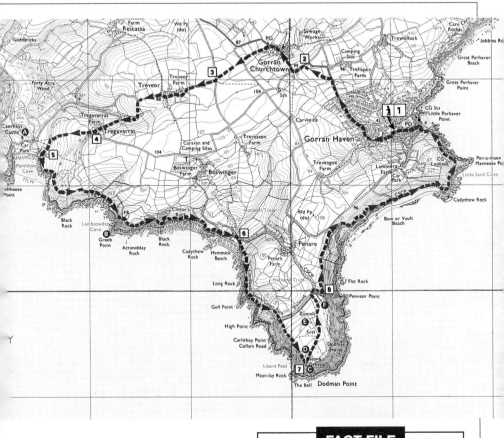

## FACT FILE

☀ Gorran Haven, 7 miles
(11.2km) south of St Austell

⌗ Pathfinder 1361 (SW 94/SX 04),
grid reference SX 010415

miles 0 1 2 3 4 5 6 7 8 9 10 miles
kms 0 1 2 3 4 5 6 7 8 9 10 11 12 13 14 15 kms

◑ Allow at least 3½ hours

▬ Good paths, strenuous ascents and
descents. Not for small children

P Car park at start (charge in summer)

🔲 Pub at Gorran Haven; cafés there
🍴 and at Caerhays in summer only

# Dangerous Dodman

*In* The Shipwreck, *JMW Turner captures the moments of fear that many sailors have experienced around the Dodman.*

Projecting headlands, treacherous rocks, submerged reefs, powerful tidal currents and foul weather driving hard from the south-west have long conspired to make the southern coast of Cornwall an internationally feared hazard for all types of shipping.

The freakishly rough waters around the Dodman – locally nicknamed 'deadman' – have claimed many vessels and lives over the centuries. Ships driven north-east by storms, past the entrance to Carrick Roads and the shelter of Falmouth's great harbour, can find it very hard to escape from Veryan Bay. It seems that almost every headland has been the scene of a maritime catastrophe.

In the early 1830s, three foreign ships were lost in the bay in one storm alone, and the terrifying speed with which they were smashed and broken up focused attention on the problems of sea rescue.

At the end of the 19th century, two naval destroyers, *Lynx* and *Thrasher*, struck the Dodman in thick fog, just below the Stone Cross. Though both ships survived, several sailors lost their lives in the incident.

Mystery still surrounds the loss of a 45-foot (14-m) cruiser, *Darlwin*, in the early 1960s. In worsening summer weather, the craft disappeared off the Dodman while returning to Mylor, near Falmouth, following a trip to Fowey, along the coast. After a search lasting several days, only a few bodies, and some traces of the *Darlwin,* were recovered; its main bulk and the bodies of most of the people on board were never found.

# Point to Point

## A coastal walk around the headlands of the Roseland Peninsula

*Looking out across Porth Creek is the attractive, colour-washed Quay Cottage.*

Unspoilt countryside and spectacular sea views are the hallmarks of this walk around the southern Roseland Peninsula. Roseland owes much of its character to its extreme position on a creek-riven spur of land at the mouth of the Carrick Roads. Its proximity to Falmouth, one of the world's greatest harbours, about a mile (1.6km) over the water to the west, is belied by the area's remote, rural calm.

The walk begins at Porth Farm and reaches the sea at Towan Beach, a sandy ribbon with rocks at low tide. Across Gerrans Bay, beyond Nare Head to the left, is Gull Rock, an island haven for a large bird colony. The path skirts low cliffs. In summer, crops reach almost to the sea.

*Continued on p. 20*➤

17

# THE WALK

## PORTH FARM–ST ANTHONY HEAD

Begin at Porth Farm car park. Turn south off the A3078 at Trewithian, signposted Gerrans, and continue straight ahead through Gerrans and Trewina.

1 Cross the road and take the shingle path signposted to the beach, under the arch on the left of the toilets. Just before the beach, turn right on the coastal path edging the low cliff and follow it past Killigerran Head and Porthmellin Head, all the way to Zone Point **Ⓐ**.

2 Go through the gap in a stone wall. Continue along the South West Coast Path onto National Trust land at St Anthony Head **Ⓑ**. Pass the battery on the left. When level with the old military cottages, turn sharp left down some wide steps signposted to the lighthouse.

3 At the bottom, where the main path leads on to the lighthouse, take the small grassy path sharp right. Pass through a gate. Further on, drop left down stone steps to cross a wooden footbridge.

Follow the waymarked path alongside a hedge, round the coast to where woods bar the way ahead.

4 Turn right uphill. Cross the stile at the top, keeping to the left of the next field as the path drops to join a track. Turn right, cross an old stone cattle-grid and follow the wooded track.

5 Where the track forks, at entrance to Place House **Ⓒ**, go right, uphill, on a wide rhodo- dendron drive. Turn left at a derelict stone building and go down steps into St Anthony's **Ⓓ**. Go through the graveyard and turn left at the exit on the road signed to Place Quay. Where the road ends, cross the stile on the right and turn left onto the field-edge path. Continue ahead, through a kissing-gate and into Drawler Plantation and continue on the path hugging the

Percuil River estuary. Follow the path as it bears right at North-hill Point and continue to an ivy-clad house, Froe. Keep to the nearside of the dammed lake. Cross a wooden footbridge on your left and turn right onto the path parallel to the road. This emerges at the grassy lower car park of Porth Farm. Head to the far left side and turn left on the road to the main car park.

### Nature Facts

**Bluebells.** If you see them in a hedge, it can mean an ancient wood once stood there.

**Money spiders.** These crea- tures spin a hammock-like web to trap unwary insects.

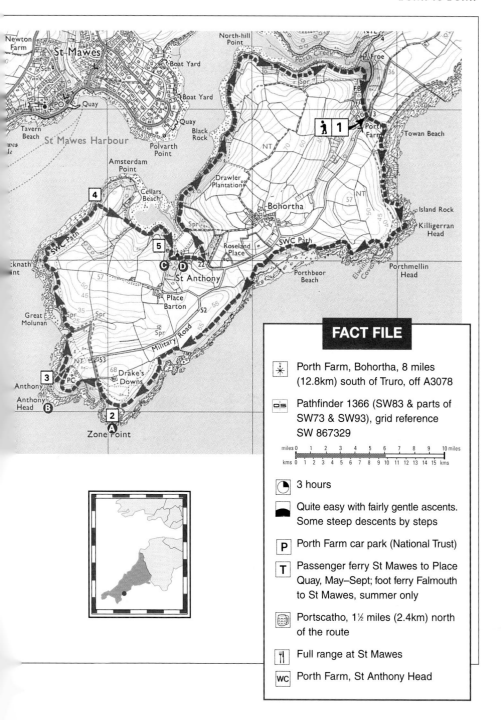

**FACT FILE**

☀ Porth Farm, Bohortha, 8 miles (12.8km) south of Truro, off A3078

⊡ Pathfinder 1366 (SW83 & parts of SW73 & SW93), grid reference SW 867329

miles 0  1  2  3  4  5  6  7  8  9  10 miles
kms 0  1  2  3  4  5  6  7  8  9  10  11  12  13  14  15  kms

◕ 3 hours

◣ Quite easy with fairly gentle ascents. Some steep descents by steps

P  Porth Farm car park (National Trust)

T  Passenger ferry St Mawes to Place Quay, May–Sept; foot ferry Falmouth to St Mawes, summer only

▦ Portscatho, 1½ miles (2.4km) north of the route

♯♯ Full range at St Mawes

WC  Porth Farm, St Anthony Head

A wooden lookout post on the path to Killigerran Head is a convenient spot to stop and watch shags or the effortless flight of fulmars. Further on, the bracken-covered cliffs fall away to tiny, inaccessible inlets.

From Zone Point **A**, the views are truly stunning. To the south and east is open sea; to the west, across the estuary, the dockside cranes and castle of Falmouth; and, to the north-west, the great artery of Carrick Roads probes deep inland. Grey seals are sometimes seen here, and kitti-wakes heard, with their distinctive cry. In the summer, migrant butterflies, such as painted ladies, may be seen, alongside the more familiar species.

A grassy path winds over St Anthony Head **B**. It has been a coastal defence site since the Iron Age, and more recently has housed an artillery emplacement. The lighthouse, which is open to visitors, was built in 1834. Its lamp helps keep ships clear of The Manacles, an infamous reef six miles (9.6km) to the south.

As you walk away north, St Mawes Harbour appears ahead. The open path wends behind the scoop of Molunan Beach, past dramatic groups of pine trees, then drops steadily down to sea level under a canopy of ash and sycamore.

The large gardens of Place House **C**, facing St Mawes, run down to the waterside. Sir Samuel Spry built the present house in neo-Gothic style in 1840. The 13th-century church of St Anthony-in-Roseland **D** is joined to it. This may be because the house occupies the site where an old monastery once stood. It was built, according to legend, to mark the spot where Christ took shelter during a heavy storm. He is said to have been with his uncle, Joseph of Arimathea, who was a tin trader.

Place Quay could be the start and fin-ish point of the walk in summer, when a foot ferry from St Mawes plies regularly to and fro. St Mawes itself is accessible by ferry from Falmouth. The path follows the estuary of the Percuil River to North-hill Point. The hedgerows are rich with many ferns, mosses and flowers. Occasional orchids may be seen, and wall pennywort is common.

The last stretch takes you to Froe, a splendid ivy-clad house, fronted by what appears to be a dammed lake. This was once a millpool, filled by the tide. The path leads across a bridge back to Porth Farm.

*The route makes use of an ancient stile set in a typical Cornish stone wall.*

# Frenchman's Creek

## The haunt of smugglers and the setting of a romantic novel

*The Helford River estuary on a moonless night was once the haunt of smugglers.*

This walk is centred on the secluded wooded valley of Frenchman's Creek and includes visits to two delightful villages.

Helford **Ⓐ** is a beautiful fishing village, grouped on either bank of a creek that feeds into the Helford River. Stone cottages, some whitewashed, some rough granite, some thatched and others topped with slate roofs, clamber up the hillsides. A wooden footbridge crosses the water next to the ford; beside it is a simple boathouse with a ship's weather vane and a figurehead set in the gable end.

In summer, a ferry crosses the river from Helford Point. The steep path gives steadily improving views out over Helford, then levels out into a lane across the headland.

*Continued on p. 24*➡

21

# THE WALK

## HELFORD–MANACCAN

The walk begins at the car park in Helford **Ⓐ**.

**1** Turn right out of car park onto road, and go down hill to cross the creek on the wooden footbridge. At the end of the bridge, turn right and follow the road.

**2** Turn left up steep lane beside Well House, follow it uphill.

**3** When you reach the T-junction, turn right to cross over the cattle-grid, in the direction indicated by the signpost to Frenchman's Creek.

**4** Where the track divides, turn left. Just before the gateway and drive marked 'Private' turn left and cross the stile to join the footpath alongside Frenchman's Creek **Ⓑ**.

**5** At the head of the creek, the path follows the hill up to the left, joining a broad track coming up from the right. Continue on up the hill. At the top of the hill turn right through the gate, then right (again) at the roadway.

**6** At the T-junction turn left. Cross straight over the main road and continue to the village of Manaccan **Ⓒ**.

**7** At the T-junction at the edge of the village, turn left and continue up the hill, past the school. (Or to visit the pub, turn right at this junction. Then retrace your steps back to the junction later.) Continue straight on towards Helford.

**8** At the top of the hill, turn left by the sign 'Public footpath'; then right onto path to Helford. When you reach the road, turn left to return to the start of the walk.

### Nature Facts

***Pluteus Lutescens.*** This uncommon, yellow-stemmed fungus lives mostly on rotten beech. See it May to October.

***Galerina Mutabilis.*** A fungus that grows in crowded tufts on tree stumps. Quite common.

***Leptonia Euchroa.*** With its violet cap, this fungus is found on fallen hazel and alder. (*Fungi can be poisonous, do not eat.*)

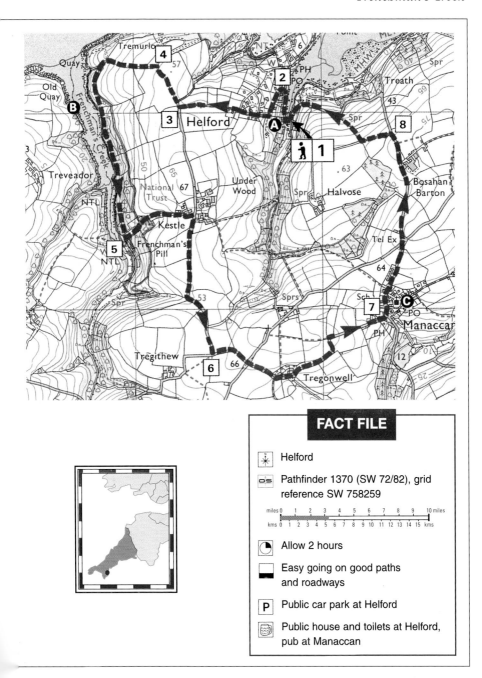

## FACT FILE

Helford

Pathfinder 1370 (SW 72/82), grid reference SW 758259

miles 0 1 2 3 4 5 6 7 8 9 10 miles

kms 0 1 2 3 4 5 6 7 8 9 10 11 12 13 14 15 kms

Allow 2 hours

Easy going on good paths and roadways

P Public car park at Helford

Public house and toilets at Helford, pub at Manaccan

Frenchman's Creek  is narrow and secluded, given a secretive air by the woodland that crowds down to the water's edge. The creek became famous as the setting for Daphne du Maurier's romantic novel of the same name.

In the 18th century it was the haunt of smugglers, and some of the houses in Helford are said to stand over secret cellars. The path begins high above the river, passing through a rough landscape of gorse and bracken with good views of the creek and river.

Frenchman's Creek at first appears as a broad inlet, but it steadily narrows and the path quite soon descends through increasingly dense woodland to the water's edge. Then the creek narrows still further, until it is little bigger than a stream. Here it is overlooked by a simple fisherman's cottage, which was restored by the Landmark Trust in 1992. The path turns sharply to take you up the hill.

As the path runs clear of the trees, it emerges into farmland where, in early spring, the fields are crowded with daffodils. At the end of the path the route moves onto a typical Cornish lane, narrow and hemmed in by high banks.

*Helford Creek is one of the most attractive fishing villages in the country.*

## The Place Of Monks

Manaccan itself  is a tight cluster of buildings, dominated by a rather grand house with a magnificent thatched roof. The village was first mentioned in AD 967 as Lesmanoc, the Place of Monks, but the church itself is later, dating from the 12th century. In the north wall there is a curious memorial dedicated to the 'Scientific Parson', the Reverend W. Gregor. In 1790 he discovered a strange black powder, which he called Menachanite, but which is now known as the light, strong metal titanium (much used in modern aircraft and ship building). The walk continues on through the village, climbing steadily until, at the top of the hill, you look down over the Helford River again.

The final part of the journey follows a path across the fields back to the steep and narrow road and eventually brings you back to the first of Helford's charming stone cottages.

24

# Lamorna Cove

## Over clifftops and past ancient monuments
## with stunning seascape views

*From Boscawen Point there are stunning views across Paynter's and St Loy's Coves.*

Lamorna Cove is an ex-fishing quay on one of West Penwith's most delightful sections of coastline. Most of the coastal section of the walk crosses the gentle seaward flanks of the surrounding countryside. It occasionally ascends to breathtaking viewpoints, but most of these are quite sheltered so you are protected from the full effects of the wind.

The most spectacular view of Lamorna Cove **Ⓐ** is from the flat-topped stone quay breakwater and harbour. In front, there is a fine view out to sea. As the path rises up to Lamorna Point, a Celtic-fashioned stone cross **Ⓑ** can be seen just below it. On the seaward side there is a faint inscription: some claim it reads 'EWW, MAY 13, 1873'. Speculation relates it to the

*Continued on p. 28*➡

25

# THE WALK

## LAMORNA COVE–LAMORNA
The walk begins on the quay wall at
Lamorna Cove **A**.

**1** Go west along quay wall to coastal path. Scramble through cluster of rocks, and take care until top of Carn Barges. Follow path past Celtic stone **B** to Lamorna Point.

**2** Path dips, and leads to Carn Barges **C**. Steps lead up to summit of rocky head. Sign points along coastal path. Follow path up hill to lane above lighthouse of Tater-du **D**.

**3** Follow lane, to pass through green gate. Cottages are above track on right, another gate is passed, and path bears left.

**4** Path descends. At bottom of dip, cross stile (beware stream hidden by undergrowth) to reach grove of bushes. Go through gate to exit left. Path rises easily at first, then steeply to Boscawen Point **E**. Pass through gate at top; follow path behind wall until opening on left takes you to stile across fence. Continue, until path levels out above cliffs. Through field, then glade of trees. Path dips to cove **F**.

**5** Turn right immediately, between beach and cliff. Pass gate, follow wall to sharp right turn. Path now follows stream (hidden in summer by vegetation). Follow bank of stream, cross bridge. Cross private drive (signpost marks coastal path), then continue to stile crossing wire fence. Turn right and ascend 100 yards (90m) until path splits. Bear right (marker post) to cross stream again. In front is a small gate; bear left here, along fence. Path comes to trees.

**6** Take path, right (at right angle); leads to drive. Follow this to gate, go through and continue through trees. Go through hamlet, and on to B3315.

**7** Turn right to Boskenna Cross **G** and continue, past Tregiffian Barrow **H** in the verge, to gate and stile on right.

**8** Follow path up hill to Merry Maidens stone circle **I**. Cross to far corner of field beyond. Hidden stile leads through boundary wall, left. Faint path leads to electricity pole in field. The Pipers **K** can be seen to left. Cross field to gap in wall; path drops to B3315.

**9** Bear right to where two lanes join road. Take cul-de-sac on left, marked Menwinnion Country House. Continue, passing Wesleyan Chapel on right, along to drive leading to Menwinnion. Take track that descends directly to surfaced road.

**10** Turn right, pass Lamorna Wink Inn to continue to Lamorna Cove and start of walk.

26

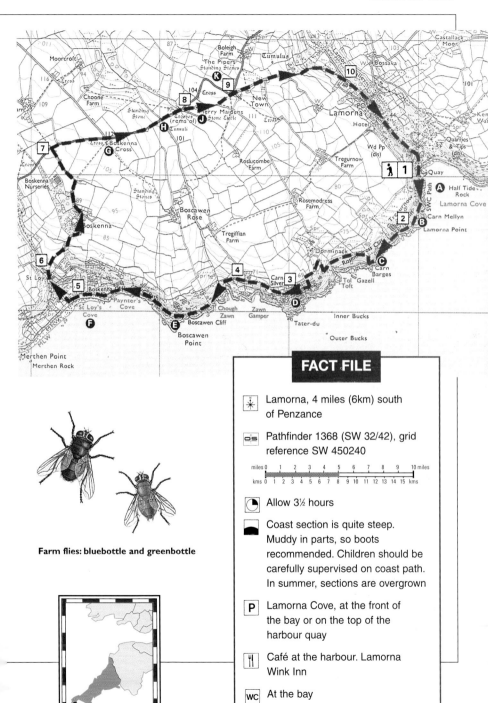

Farm flies: bluebottle and greenbottle

## FACT FILE

☀ Lamorna, 4 miles (6km) south
of Penzance

OS Pathfinder 1368 (SW 32/42), grid
reference SW 450240

| miles 0 | 1 | 2 | 3 | 4 | 5 | 6 | 7 | 8 | 9 | 10 miles |
|---|---|---|---|---|---|---|---|---|---|---|
| kms 0 | 1 2 | 3 | 4 | 5 6 | 7 | 8 | 9 10 | 11 12 | 13 14 | 15 kms |

◐ Allow 3½ hours

■ Coast section is quite steep.
Muddy in parts, so boots
recommended. Children should be
carefully supervised on coast path.
In summer, sections are overgrown

P Lamorna Cove, at the front of
the bay or on the top of the
harbour quay

🍴 Café at the harbour. Lamorna
Wink Inn

WC At the bay

wrecking of the *Garonne* in May 1868, when the bodies of two young girls were washed ashore.

The rocky pinnacled summit of Carn Barges ❻ offers an excellent view across to the lighthouse ❼ standing above the cliffs of Tater-du.

Crowning the summit of Boscawen Point ❽, there is an impressive jumble of granite pinnacles and blocks. In the breeding season, a colony of herring gulls will be visible just across the top of the cliff. Down the hill and past the meadow, a glade of stunted oaks offers dappled shade, and next, by way of a contrast, St Loy's Cove ❾ presents a good array of giant crystalline rock.

**Granite Monuments**

After passing Boskenna, the road leads rapidly to the St Buryan junction. On the right is the distinctive Boskenna Cross ❿. This walk passes some interesting megalithic monuments. On a widened verge a little further along the road, close inspection of a pile of granite blocks reveals a structure rather like a tomb; this is Tregiffian Barrow ⓗ.

Further on, the Merry Maidens stone circle ⓙ dates from 2500–1500 BC. In the fields beyond, The Pipers ⓚ are two tall granite standing stones positioned 100 yards (90m) apart. They are said to be the largest standing stones in Cornwall.

*Nature Facts*

**Herring gull.** The typical seagull of resorts and fish quays, this is a large, 23-inch (57-cm) bird that lays its eggs on grassy patches on cliff ledges.

**Lesser black-backed gull.** A large, 22-inch (58-cm) bird, this gull is widespread in summer, breeding in colonies on islands and moors.

**Common tern.** This slim, 14-inch (36-cm) bird has a glossy black cap in summer. It lays 2 to 4 dappled eggs in an unlined scrape.

# At the Edge of Land's End

## A coastal walk along the most westerly tip of Britain

*The cliffs fall into the sea at Land's End, called* Belerion *(Seat Of Storms) by the Romans.*

Land's End is a focal point for many tourists. This walk enables you to get away from the crowds and discover one of the best hidden sandy bays in Cornwall, complete with swimming, paddling and rock pools. Along the way there is breath-taking coastal cliff scenery, with rocky islands and headlands, and magnificent views to the great Atlantic beyond.

There are ancient field systems, fascinating old mines, wreckers' coves and smugglers' caves, and finally the unspoilt sandy bay of Nanjizal – a perfect place to swim or relax and have a picnic.

Out to sea, looking beyond the granite cliffs that mark the beginning and end of our island, stands man's last bastion – the famous Longships Lighthouse. This section

*Continued on p. 32*➤

# THE WALK

## LAND'S END–NANJIZAL BAY
The large car park and complex at Land's End provides the starting point for this walk.

1 Join the coastal path at Britain's first and last signpost in front of the hotel above the cliffs. Follow the coastal path south. Initially this runs along near the edge of the cliffs. Despite various commercial developments, including a miniature village, standing on the first few hundred yards, the path is a public right of way. It is part of the Cornwall Coast Path, and is well signposted.

2 Once beyond the man-made attractions of Land's End, the well-defined path moves inland slightly. The rocky island known as the Armed Knight **A** appears on the right and is followed by the spectacular island (when the tide is in) and the sea arch of Enys Dodnan **B**. Shortly after this a smaller footpath branches off right from the main track.

Follow this towards the coast and a large headland. This is known as Pordenack Point **C** and is reached ½ mile (800m) from the start.

3 From this point the footpath continues circuitously to return to the main coastal route. Continue on the coastal path until two granite pinnacle blocks stand on the right. After these, lose height slightly to cross a small valley and then follow a narrower path that veers off right from the main path. Continue out to the headland beyond. Marked simply as Carn Boel **D** on the map, this is actually a dual headland, Carn Sperm to the north and Carn Boel to the south, separated by a deep, precipitous sea-filled rift in the cliffs known as a 'zawn'. Do not attempt to look over into the zawn.

4 The path again moves inland and soon rejoins the main coast path to descend, passing through a network of ancient field systems with stone walls constructed from granite blocks. There is a stile where the path rejoins the edge of the coast, and you overlook Nanjizal Bay at its northern end. There are sea caves in this cove, known as Zawn Reeth **E**.

5 The path above the bay is well defined but quite narrow; it cuts through granite cliffs, past a mine entrance on the left (do not go in, as it's dangerous). You reach a tiny stream, which feeds into the beautiful, unspoilt Nanjizal Bay **F**. Cross the footbridge into the bay.

The return route follows the main coastal path, keeping inland, to Carn Boel/Carn Sperm, then to Pordenack Point.

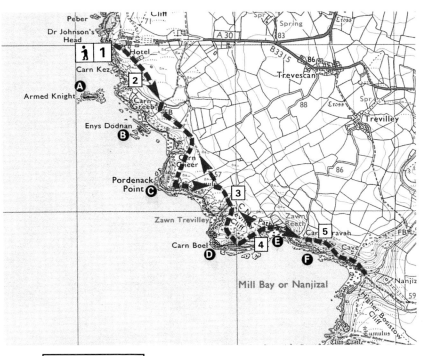

Types of sedge: (l–r) pale, common yellow and common sedge

of Land's End is known as Dr Johnson's Head, and on the steep cliffs immediately below there is a classic rock climb known as the Land's End Long Climb. For experts only, it was pioneered by the Royal Marines, who still use it for training.

Although it is virtually submerged when heavy seas are running, at low tide the distinctive rocky island of the Armed Knight ❶ provides a home for gulls and food for hungry oystercatchers. The spectacular sea arch that tunnels through Enys Dodnan ❷ is a fine example of the immense power of the sea. Some time in the future, the roof of the arch will collapse and leave a solitary finger of rock, remote from the main island, forming a sea stack.

**Coastal Views**

Arguably, Pordenack Point ❸ provides the most advantageous view of Land's End, the cliffs and Longships Lighthouse. The artist Turner painted from this headland. The next rocky point along the coast is the headland of Carn Sperm and Carn Boel ❹. Moving on, with the headland providing protection to the west, there is an ancient field system, with stone walls made from large blocks. Curiously arranged at intervals along the tops of the terraced walls are standing stones, placed upright. Their origin is unknown. After passing these, you arrive at the spot that overlooks Zawn Reeth ❺.

This cove forms the northern end of Nanjizal Bay ❻. Below, the cliffs are crumbling from the onslaught of the waves. When the tide is out a boulder beach leads to the sea. Forming the back of the zawn are cliffs, honeycombed with sea tunnels that years ago may have been used as smugglers' caves.

**Sandy Bay**

The head of the bay is the only place where walkers should go down to the sea. Nanjizal, its Cornish name, is preferable to the dull alternative, Mill Bay. Here you can swim or paddle – but only when the sea is warm and calm, and the tide is incoming.

*Nature Facts*

**Red Admiral butterfly** (top). These arrive in flocks in spring, from hotter climes. **Brimstone butterflies** (male above, female below). They hibernate in winter.

# Atlantic Headland

## Cliff walking on the dramatic
## north-west Cornish peninsula

*Gurnard's Head stretches into the Atlantic. Unusually for this area, the rock is greenstone.*

The West Penwith region of Cornwall is famed for its rugged coastline and colourful history. This walk goes through fields towards the coast. The route passes through an area where rich natural resources were once harvested: tin and copper from the rock, pilchards from the sea. After crossing the coastal path, Gurnard's Head (regarded as one of the most striking promontories in Cornwall) provides the highlight of the walk, offering superlative views of this wild and dramatic coastline.

The early part of the walk goes through the hamlet of Treen to gain open, treeless fields leading towards Gurnard's Head. Before the coastal path is reached, it is possible to see the mine workings **Ⓐ** that

*Continued on p. 36*➤

33

# THE WALK

## TREEN–GURNARD'S HEAD
The walk begins at the Gurnard's Head Hotel.

**1** From the hotel, follow lane into Treen.

**2** Before you reach the end of the hamlet, a path defined by a post and wire fence turns off left. Follow this, between two garage-like buildings (these were once a coastguard housing station). Climb the stile, which is constructed from granite slabs, to reach open fields. Cross these via a further stile and gate. You can follow most of the row of telegraph poles that points directly to Gurnard's Head.

**3** The fields soon give way to rougher ground, and the coastal path. Down to the right, mine workings **A** can be seen and a long building (the Old Pilchard Factory **B**) on the edge of Lean Point. Cross the coastal path to follow the narrow path along to Gurnard's Head **C**.

**4** From Gurnard's Head there are several paths up the hillside. Follow the map carefully and retrace your steps as the map shows. Turn right to follow the coastal path that crosses the cliffs of Carn Gloose **D**, the small headlands of Robin's Rocks **E** and Porthmeor Point **F** before gently descending into Porthmeor Cove.

**5** Go through the clearing to reach the stream. After crossing the stream, bear left to follow the path above the stream up the valley.

**6** Pass the old mine buildings **G**, then fork left to recross the stream and continue to Lower Porthmeor Farm.

**7** Walk through the farm and across the lane to follow the path leading through two fields. Turn left to the road, and return to the Gurnard's Head Hotel.

### Nature Facts

**Black Darter.** This dragonfly flies restlessly, continually returning to the same place. It favours marshy, boggy areas.

**Four-spotted chaser.** With a dark spot on each of its four wings, this dragonfly is common throughout the British Isles.

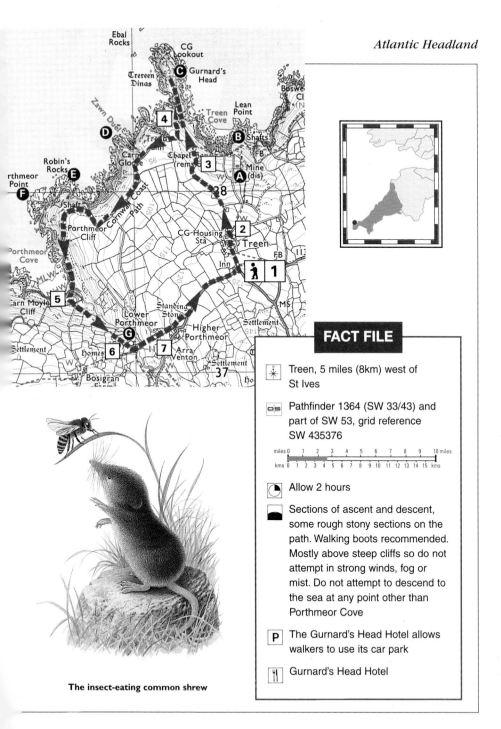

**FACT FILE**

☀ Treen, 5 miles (8km) west of St Ives

⊡ Pathfinder 1364 (SW 33/43) and part of SW 53, grid reference SW 435376

miles 0 1 2 3 4 5 6 7 8 9 10 miles
kms 0 1 2 3 4 5 6 7 8 9 10 11 12 13 14 15 kms

◐ Allow 2 hours

▬ Sections of ascent and descent, some rough stony sections on the path. Walking boots recommended. Mostly above steep cliffs so do not attempt in strong winds, fog or mist. Do not attempt to descend to the sea at any point other than Porthmeor Cove

🅿 The Gurnard's Head Hotel allows walkers to use its car park

🍴 Gurnard's Head Hotel

**The insect-eating common shrew**

tumble down to Lean Head on the east side of Treen Cove. The long building above the sea is known as the Old Pilchard Factory **B**. Pilchards, once locally known as 'fair maids', were the basis of a flourishing industry in the past.

The Catholic observance of not eating meat on Fridays ensured a thriving export trade of pilchards, preserved in salt, to the Mediterranean. In those times a toast of the St Ives fishermen, 'Long life to the Pope, death to our best friends and may our streets run in blood' (the 'best friends' being the pilchards), started the season.

Standing proud against the Atlantic rollers, the tip of Gurnard's Head **C** rises to form a distinctive bump of naked greenstone. It takes its name from a fish that is common in these waters. It also has a Cornish name, Trereen Dinas, or 'the castle on the high place', which refers to the castle sited here.

**Ancient Earthworks**

On the sheltered eastern slopes of the headland, the remains of 18 hut circles have been found - these now take the shape of circular grassy platforms. The tip of the promontory can be visited easily,

*Rock samphire grows on shingle, cliffs, rocks and sand.*

but its rocky head is a difficult scramble, only recommended for the experienced.

Walking from the head to the cliffs is quite strenuous, though the coastal path is soon reached and the going almost flat. Looking back to the cliff of Carn Gloose **D** provides a breathtaking sight, for the rocks plunge vertically 200 feet (60m) into the sea. The headlands of Robin's Rocks **E** and Porthmeor Point **F** are not so steep. Their ledges provide a preening point and home for shags and cormorants.

The rocky shore of the cove marks a change in character, for here the darker angular greenstone (which is actually jet black) gives way to the more rounded pink-red granite.

A bridge leads across the stream before the path climbs to some old ruined mine buildings **G** – now easier to see since the land has been cleared by the National Trust. They were once used to process tin ore from the nearby Carn Galver mine. They comprise water-wheel pits, stamping pits and circular buddles (the bases for the revolving brushes which separated the crushed ore from the rock). The mine closed in 1871. Above this relic of times past, the path crosses the stream to rise to Lower Porthmeor Farm.

# In Search of Camelot

## From a coastal village to castle ruins linked with legend

*Tintagel Castle is the legendary seat of King Arthur, although the building is medieval.*

Dramatic Tintagel Head, protected by cliffs and bearing the ruins of a castle, seems the ideal setting for the court of Camelot. Tintagel has therefore been connected with the Arthurian legend.

Attention was first focused on the area when Turner painted Tintagel Head in 1819. Interest grew in 1842 when Tennyson wrote his poems 'Morte d'Arthur'

and 'Idylls of the King'. The legend peaked at the end of the 19th century, after the arrival of the railway at Camelford in 1893 had opened the area to tourists.

There is no real evidence to show that this site has any connection with King Arthur. But it was once an important defensive position. This walk not only explores Tintagel Head but also visits

*Continued on p. 40*➤

# THE WALK

## TINTAGEL–TINTAGEL HEAD

The walk begins at the large car park on the main street of Tintagel.

**1** Turn right out of the car park, then cross the road to turn left down Church Hill Road to Tintagel's church **Ⓐ**.

**2** From the church head south down the coast, bearing right on a path leading first to the Old Golf Course and then to the Youth Hostel. Continue behind this, descending slightly to Dunderhole Point. From here it is possible to see Gull Point Quarry **Ⓑ** across Lambhouse Cove.

**3** Retrace your steps to the Youth Hostel, then follow the coastal path north. Pass Long Grass Quarry **Ⓒ** in the cliffs below, and continue until you can descend to the wooden bridge between Tintagel Head **Ⓓ** and the mainland. Tintagel Haven forms a naturally protected harbour and the beach is reached by some steps.

**4** You will need to pay to cross the bridge, before you ascend the steps to enter a wooden door in the wall of Tintagel Castle **Ⓔ**.

**5** Continue through the remains of the castle to exit through an arch in the far wall. Pass a hut, then take the track rising to the left. Follow this track to the summit of Tintagel Head. A path descends in a clockwise direction, and leads back to the arch in the castle wall. Return to the bridge. Cross it and follow the road back into the village, where you can return to the car park.

*Nature Facts*

**Carragheen/Irish moss.** This common seaweed grows thickest near the low water mark.

**Gut weed.** The intestine-like hollow fronds of this seaweed are found near fresh-water outflows.

**Cladophora rupestris.** This sea plant is prolific in summer.

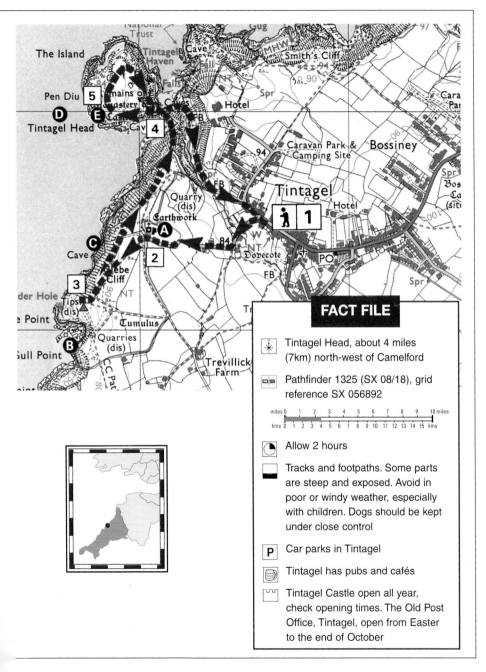

other interesting sites, including some abandoned slate quarry workings.

Tintagel village is generally very busy in the summer months. It is an easy stroll down Church Hill to Tintagel's church **Ⓐ**, dedicated to St Materiana. It is possibly Norman, but unusually the tower rises from its west end. Inside there is a Roman milestone (AD 250) in the south transept and a Norman font and windows. In the churchyard some of the headstones are buttressed by stones against the strong westerly gales.

The Post Office dates from the 14th century, and is based on the plan of a medieval manor house. Now it has been restored and is owned by the National Trust.

There is a coastal path leading above Glebe Cliff which goes through the Old Golf Course. Below the Youth Hostel is Gull Point Slate Quarry **Ⓑ**. This was last worked in the 1920s, when men were lowered from the cliff top to work the beds of slate. The disused Longhouse Quarry and Lambhouse Quarry are nearby.

Across from the lip of Long Grass Quarry **Ⓒ** is a large cave, enlarged by the quarrymen. In the fragments of slate, look out for the 'Delabole butterfly', a fossil that

*The Post Office in the centre of Tintagel started receiving letters in Victorian times.*

resembles a Manta Ray. In fact, it is a shellfish that was buried in the mud that formed the slates 350 million years ago.

**Natural Harbour**

Along the coast, extensive bird life can be observed. Fulmars glide along the tops of the cliffs, where guillemots, razorbills and shags all nest.

On the rocks sea lavender and rock samphire grow. The latter is a fleshy plant with a distinct salty taste - it was once a common food, eaten pickled or fresh.

Many small sailing vessels once frequented Tintagel Haven, a naturally protected harbour. Coal was unloaded, slate taken away, and the boats 'hobbled' (part rowed and part pulled by ropes) in and out of the haven.

Tintagel Castle **Ⓔ**, situated on Tintagel Head **Ⓕ**, was built in the 12th and 13th centuries. It is reached via a hanging footbridge and steep stone steps.

From the summit of Tintagel Head there are fine views and a sense of its defensive position. The site was certainly a pre-Norman trading settlement or stronghold. It is a good place for a picnic before taking the track back to the castle.

# Heritage Coast

## A walk combining the most attractive elements of Cornish scenery

*The rocky beach at Duckpool is typical of the North Cornish coast.*

Duckpool, where the walk begins, is a little rocky bay, seen at its most dramatic in rough weather when the waves crash against the cliffs. The first part of the walk follows the long-distance coastal path and begins with a steep climb to the top of the cliffs. The path itself is narrow and rocky, but the effort of climbing is well rewarded by magnificent views along the coast. There is also an intriguing view of the vast, white dishes of the satellite tracking station **A**.

### Windswept Coast

Beyond this point is an area of coarse grass and heather; the bird population includes many stone chats, swooping low over the bushes. Field boundaries consist

*Continued on p. 44*➤

41

# THE WALK

## DUCKPOOL–COOMBE

The walk starts at the National Trust car park at Duckpool.

1 Looking out to sea, turn right onto the path leading up to the top of the cliffs. Having reached the top of the climb, follow the signs marked 'Coastal Path'. Continue past the satellite tracking station **A** on your right, following the signposts until you arrive at Stanbury Mouth.

2 After descending from the cliffs, cross the footbridge over the stream. Turn right to follow the stream in the direction indicated by the arrow 'Footpath Inland'.

3 Where the path divides, do not cross the stile, but continue on the lane as it swings round to the left. At the top of the lane, turn right on to the road.

4 Where the road bends round to the left by the farm buildings, turn right by the name plate 'Stanbury Manor Morlyn Welsh Cobs' **B**. Turn left onto the stony footpath between two ponds. Go through the gate and follow the path round to the right, as indicated by the yellow arrow. Head for the stile by the telegraph pole. Continue to follow the waymark arrows.

5 Cross straight over the road and take the path by the sign 'Public Footpath', again clearly waymarked by yellow arrows.

6 At the roadway in Woodford village, turn right. At the end of the 30 mph zone, the road turns left - continue on the road marked as a dead end, and beyond Shears Farm turn right onto the broad track signposted 'Public Footpath'.

7 At the rim of the wooded valley, there are yellow arrows to follow down the hill. The route immediately divides; take the path down to the right. Cross the stream on the footbridge, then cross the stile and turn right. Continue along the well-defined path.

8 At the roadway turn right and continue along the road through the hamlet of Coombe **C**. At the T-junction turn left, then right onto the road, which is signposted to Duckpool. Return to the start of the walk.

*Nature Facts*

**Orb-web spider.** This spider's web gives the creature its name.

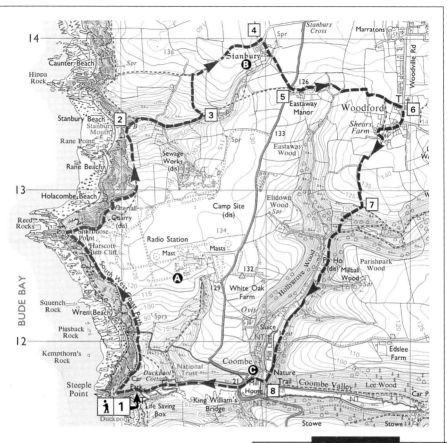

## FACT FILE

⊛ Coombe, Cornwall, 4 miles (6½km) north of Bude, off A39

▱ Pathfinder 1273 (SS 21/31), grid reference SS 201116

miles 0 1 2 3 4 5 6 7 8 9 10 miles
kms 0 1 2 3 4 5 6 7 8 9 10 11 12 13 14 15 kms

◗ Allow 3 hours

▬ The walk may be muddy in places and the initial climb is steep. Walking shoes are recommended

P Car park at Duckpool, on coast, 3 miles (5km) north of Bude

of low stone walls built into earthen banks topped by shrubs distorted by the wind.

The descent from the cliff-top walk is comparatively gentle, leading to a grassy path beside a stream. This soon becomes a green lane, stony underfoot and running between banks and hedgerows – the upper part of the lane is bordered by dense clusters of blackberry bushes.

There is a brief interlude of walking down a roadway, then you reach Stanbury Manor Farm ❸, obviously an old manor house with its solid stone walls and massive chimneys. The path leads through the farm grounds, past an ornamental lily pond, then through the fields to the village of Eastaway. This too was once the site of a manor house, but the village, a mixture of old and new picturesque thatched cottages and stone farmhouses, has sprung up in its place.

*The mill at Coombe was used for sawing timber on the Stowe Barton Estate.*

Here you follow another lane, and this opens out into a path across the fields to Woodford. This path leads across the fields before descending steeply through woodland to the river valley.

The valley is an area of broad-leaved wood, dominated by birch, with a spattering of oak and sycamore. A busy little stream forms an accompaniment to the walk. Soon the path opens out and you reach the hamlet of Coombe ❸.

**Great Estates**

All this area was once part of the great Stowe Barton estate, which belonged to the Grenville family. Its most famous member was Sir Richard Grenville, who, as captain of the *Revenge*, fought the Spaniards off the Azores in 1591. The Grenvilles were instrumental in restoring Charles II to the throne and, as a reward, Sir John Grenville was made Earl of Bath. His great house has now gone, but the estates survive.

The old water mill, once used to grind corn and work a saw mill, still stands. For a time Coombe was the home of the Reverend Stephen Hawker of Morwenstow, who stayed in a cottage (Hawker's Cottage) just across the ford. He is best remembered as the founder of the Harvest Festival service.

Finally the road goes through a ford, but walkers can keep dry by crossing the footbridge. For the last part of the walk, the valley broadens out as the river flows down to the sea at Duckpool.

# Index